A Trip to the Trains

by Pamela Thilo
illustrated by Albert Molnar

Orlando   Boston   Dallas   Chicago   San Diego

Mrs. Gray teaches at Bay School.
Last week her class went on a
field trip to see some trains.

Mr. Ray drove the bus to the railroad yard. On the way, the class went past the bay.

"Look, class," said Mrs. Gray.
"There are eight sailboats sailing
in the bay. What a good day
for sailing!"

Then the bus drove down Main
Road to the railroad yard. The
class got off. Mr. Ray waited on
the bus by the Day Parking sign.

The class looked at a lot of
trains. Some were plain, gray
trains. Other trains had pictures
painted on them.

Some trains were old. They were
steam trains. These days, they
stayed in the railroad yard.

Other trains were new and
fast. They could sail down the
railroad tracks.

The class hiked on a trail to
some old tracks by the bay. The
same eight sailboats were still
sailing in the breeze.

Soon it was time to go back to
school. The class climbed back
onto the bus. Mr. Ray started
to drive.

Then rain started to fall. "I'm glad
the rain waited," said Mrs. Gray.
"We stayed dry!"

The bus went past the bay.
The boats were not sailing in the
rain. The children didn't mind.
They were thinking about trains.